# GUITAR
# REFERENCE
# GUIDE

# EXERCISES

## BY JOE CHARUPAKORN

ISBN 1-57560-402-7

Copyright © 2001 CHERRY LANE MUSIC COMPANY
International Copyright Secured     All Rights Reserved

The music, text, design and graphics in this publication are protected by copyright law.
Any duplication or transmission, by any means, electronic, mechanical, photocopying,
recording or otherwise, is an infringement of copyright.

*Visit our website at www.cherrylane.com*

# PREFACE

Technical studies are an important part of every musician's development. This book presents a wide variety of exercises for guitar—with several fingering options for each—designed to enhance not only your technical ability, but also your fretboard visualization skills.

In addition to the exercises, there are three pieces from the classical violin repertoire in the last section of this book that will give you a truly challenging technical workout: The allegro assai from J.S. Bach's Sonata #5 for solo violin, *Moto Perpetuo* by Paganinni, and Wohlfahrt's Study #3.

This book is a good source for practice material and makes a perfect companion to the *Guitar Reference Guide Scales* and *Arpeggios* books.

—Joe Charupakorn

# ABOUT THE AUTHOR

Joe Charupakorn is a guitarist, composer, and author. He earned a Masters of Fine Arts in Composition from Purchase Conservatory of Music at the State University of New York where he graduated Magna Cum Laude. Joe has also studied privately with many musical heavyweights, including jazz pianists Richie Beirach and Mike Longo, guitar legend Mike Stern, and contemporary classical composer Ruth Schonthal. He lives in New York City, where he is active as a performer, composer, and teacher.

# ACKNOWLEDGMENTS

I'd like to thank Arthur Rotfeld and Nick Russo, my editors, for their input, insight, and patience, and my parents (Chavalit and Boonchit), Sup, and all of my friends for their support.

This book is dedicated to my mother.

# CONTENTS

# INTRODUCTION

The best way to use this book is to create a practice strategy. This means choosing a few exercises (you don't have to learn *every* exercise in the book) and working on them daily until you feel you have technically mastered them.

A good practice routine consists of starting out with some of the warm-up exercises, to get the blood flowing, then taking a scale pattern and playing through each fingering of the pattern. Do this slowly and try to visualize the shapes of the scales as you play the pattern. Work on the arpeggio patterns in a similar fashion.

Learn each exercise with all the fingerings given slowly and carefully, never sacrificing clarity and accuracy for speed. The goal is to develop an instinctive command of the fretboard.

A metronome is a good tool to help chart your progress—be sure to get one if you don't already have one. Use it to keep track of tempo markings daily to monitor your progress. See what tempos you are comfortable with and what your upper limits are.

# HOW TO USE THIS BOOK

This book is arranged as follows: First a presentation of the scales and arpeggios with several fingering options, then exercises based on these fingerings. Learn each fingering of the scales and arpeggios thoroughly before attempting the exercises. Try learning one scale and one arpeggio exercise per week and you will notice a significant improvement in your technical ability.

At the end of the book are some etudes from the masters that will prove to be an extreme technical challenge. Don't be intimidated by these pieces; with consistent practice you will be able to play them. Start slowly, building up speed daily and using your metronome as a guide.

## Warm-Up Exercises

The warm-up exercises consist of the 24 finger patterns possible using a one-finger-per-fret finger pattern scheme in first position. Keep your left hand fingers as close to the fretboard as possible to economize the finger movements (especially the pinky and ring finger).

## Scales

The exercises in this book are based on the three most common scales—the major scale, the ascending or jazz melodic minor scale, and the harmonic minor scale. Four fingerings are given: fifth-position, seventh-position, eighth-position, and a three-notes-per-string fingering.

## Scale Sequences

The scale sequences are based on the three scales and the four fingerings given. Study each fingering of the patterns and see how they relate to each other.

## Arpeggios

All arpeggios from triads to seventh chords are presented with four different fingerings, just like the scales. These fingerings are the most common fingerings and should be memorized.

## Arpeggio Sequences

The arpeggio sequences are based on the four arpeggio fingerings presented in the arpeggios section.

## Diatonic Arpeggio Sequences

Diatonic arpeggio sequences are presented in the key of C major. After learning them in C major, try these patterns using the C jazz melodic minor and C harmonic minor scales as a resource. Practice them in other keys as well.

## Linear Diatonic Arpeggios

Linear arpeggios move horizontally across the fretboard rather than the position-based vertical fingerings presented earlier and are shown here in the key of C major (again, after learning them in C, try using the C jazz melodic minor and C harmonic minor). Learning these linear arpeggios will help solidify your knowledge of the fretboard and improve your technique.

## Pieces

As a conclusion to the book, three challenging pieces from the violin repertoire are presented. The Allegro Assai from J.S. Bach's Sonata #5 for solo violin, Paganini's *Moto Perpetuo,* and Wohlfahrt's Study #3.

# Warm-up Exercises

## #1

## #2

# Warm-up Exercises

## #3

## #4

# Warm-up Exercises

## #5

## #6

# Warm-up Exercises

## #7

## #8

# Warm-up Exercises

## #9

## #10

# Warm-up Exercises

## #11

## #12

# Warm-up Exercises

## #13

## #14

# Warm-up Exercises

## #15

## #16

# Warm-up Exercises

## #17

## #18

# Warm-up Exercises

## #19

## #20

# Warm-up Exercises

## #21

## #22

# Warm-up Exercises

## #23

## #24

# Exercise #1: C Major Scale

## Fingering #1

## Fingering #2

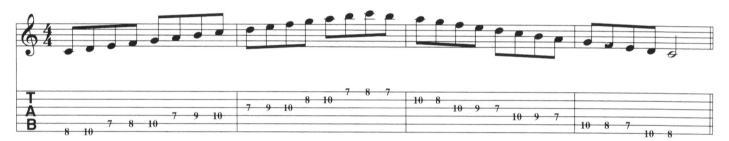

## Fingering #3

## Fingering #4

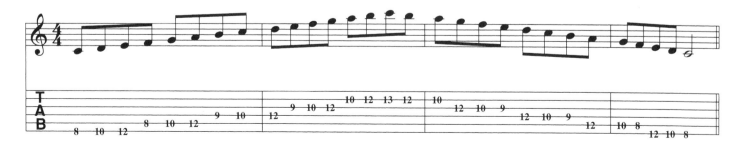

# Exercise #2: C Jazz Melodic Minor Scale

## Fingering #1

## Fingering #2

## Fingering #3

## Fingering #4

# Exercise #3: C Harmonic Minor Scale

## Fingering #1

## Fingering #2

## Fingering #3

## Fingering #4

# Exercise #4: C Chromatic Scale

# Exercise #5: Scale Sequence in C Major

## Fingering #1

## Fingering #2

# Exercise #5: Scale Sequence in C Major

## Fingering #3

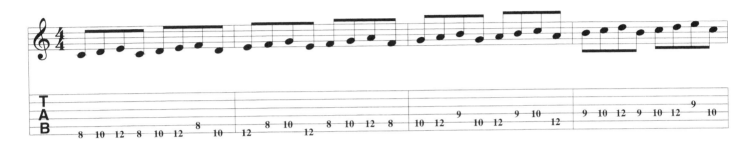

## Fingering #4

# Exercise #6: Scale Sequence in C Melodic Minor

## Fingering #1

## Fingering #2

# Exercise #6: Scale Sequence in C Melodic Minor

## Fingering #3

## Fingering #4

# Exercise #7: Scale Sequence in C Harmonic Minor

## Fingering #1

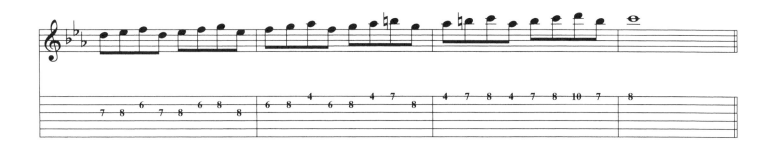

## Fingering #2

# Exercise #7: Scale Sequence in C Harmonic Minor

## Fingering #3

## Fingering #4

# Exercise #8: Scale Sequence in C Major

## Fingering #1

## Fingering #2

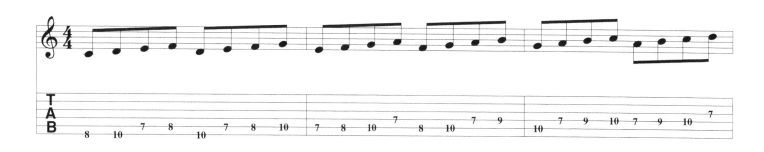

# Exercise #8: Scale Sequence in C Major

## Fingering #3

## Fingering #4

# Exercise #9: Scale Sequence in C Jazz Melodic Minor

## Fingering #1

## Fingering #2

# Exercise #9: Scale Sequence in C Jazz Melodic Minor

## Fingering #3

## Fingering #4

# Exercise #10: Scale Sequence in C Harmonic Minor

## Fingering #1

## Fingering #2

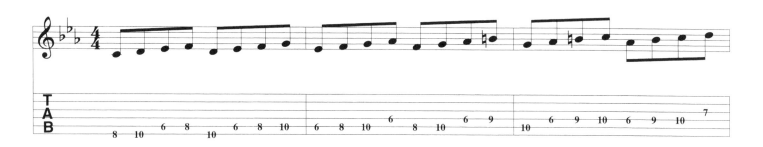

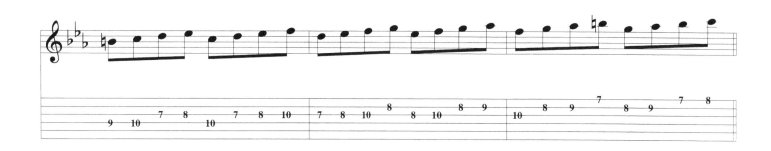

# Exercise #10: Scale Sequence in C Harmonic Minor

## Fingering #3

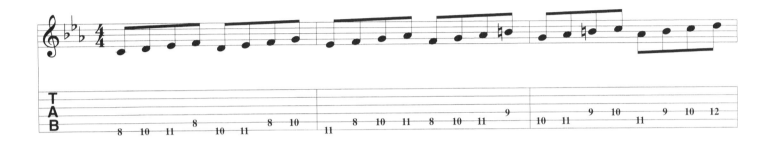

## Fingering #4

# Exercise #11: Scale Sequence in C Major

## Fingering #1

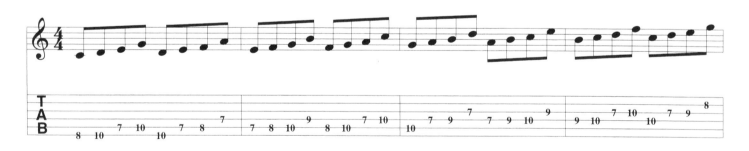

## Fingering #2

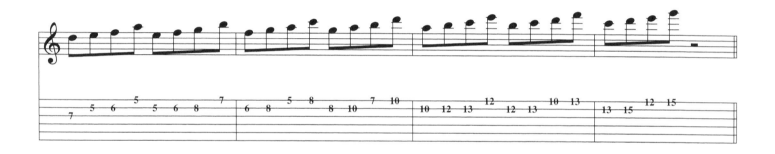

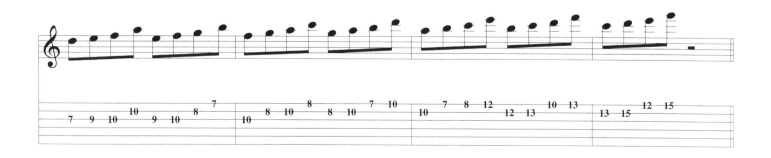

# Exercise #11: Scale Sequence in C Major

## Fingering #3

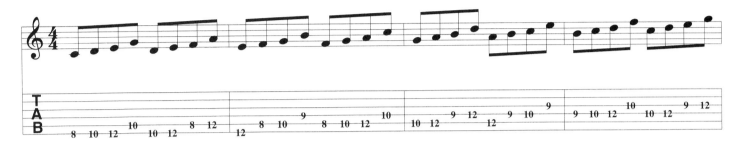

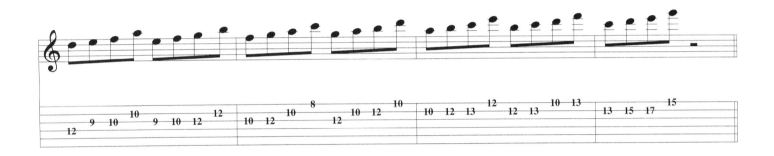

## Fingering #4

# Exercise #12: Scale Sequence in C Jazz Melodic Minor

## Fingering #1

## Fingering #2

# Exercise #12: Scale Sequence in C Jazz Melodic Minor

## Fingering #3

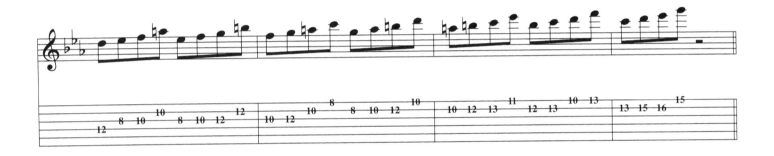

## Fingering #4

# Exercise #13: Scale Sequence in C Harmonic Minor

## Fingering #1

## Fingering #2

# Exercise #13: Scale Sequence in C Harmonic Minor

## Fingering #3

## Fingering #4

# Exercise #14: Scale Sequence in C Major

## Fingering #1

## Fingering #2

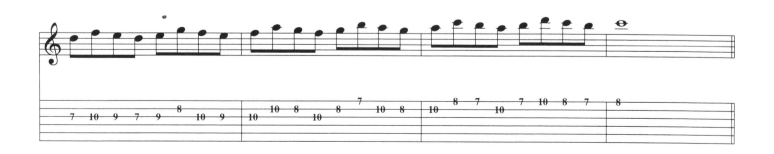

# Exercise #14: Scale Sequence in C Major

## Fingering #3

## Fingering #4

# Exercise #15: Scale Sequence in C Jazz Melodic Minor

## Fingering #1

## Fingering #2

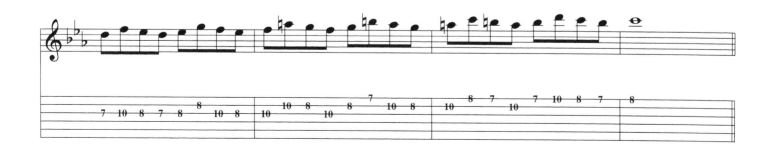

# Exercise #15: Scale Sequence in C Jazz Melodic Minor

## Fingering #3

## Fingering #4

# Exercise #16: Scale Sequence in C Harmonic Minor

## Fingering #1

## Fingering #2

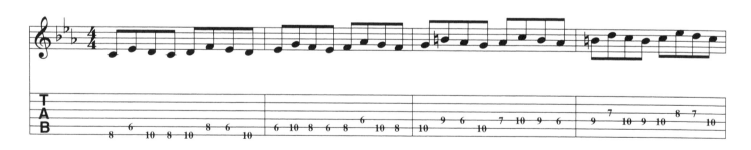

# Exercise #16: Scale Sequence in C Harmonic Minor

## Fingering #3

## Fingering #4

# Exercise #17: Scale Sequence in C Major

## Fingering #1

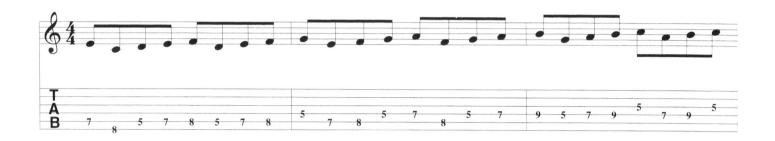

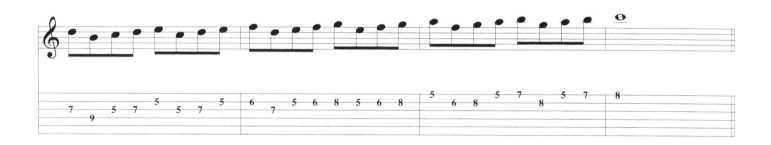

## Fingering #2

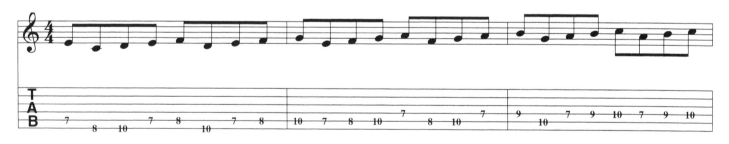

# Exercise #17: Scale Sequence in C Major

## Fingering #3

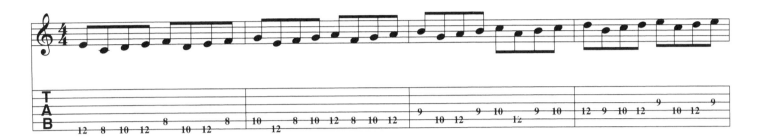

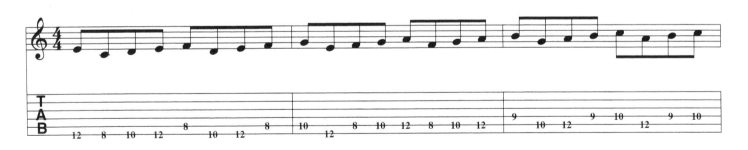

## Fingering #4

# Exercise #18: Scale Sequence in C Jazz Melodic Minor

## Fingering #1

## Fingering #2

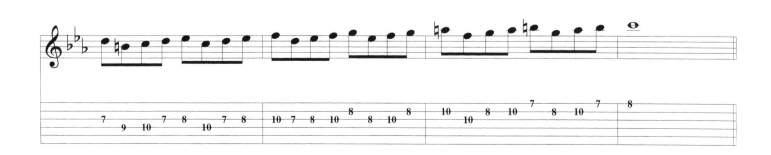

# Exercise #18: Scale Sequence in C Jazz Melodic Minor

## Fingering #3

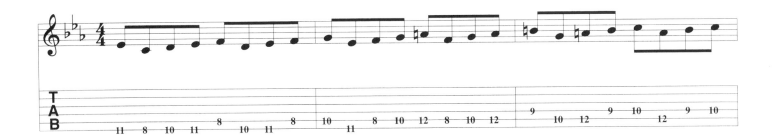

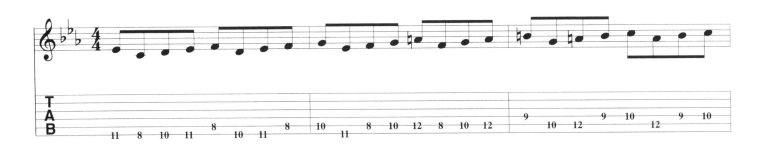

## Fingering #4

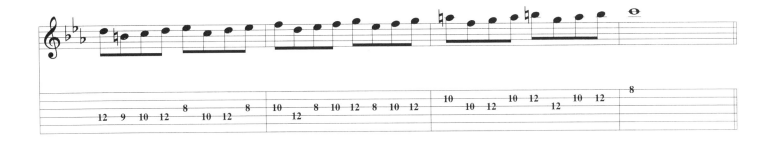

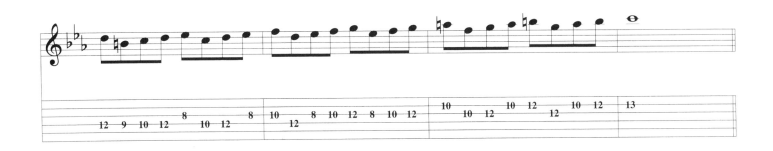

# Exercise #19: Scale Sequence in C Harmonic Minor

## Fingering #1

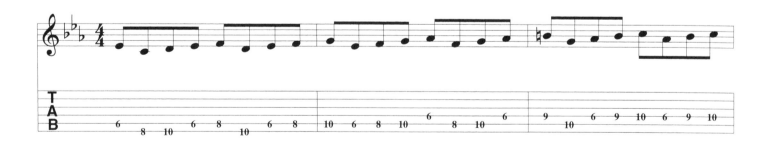

## Fingering #2

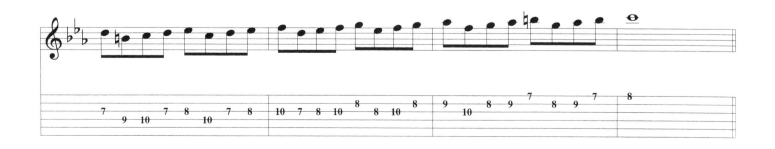

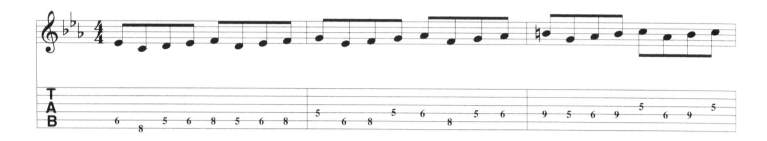

# Exercise #19: Scale Sequence in C Harmonic Minor

## Fingering #3

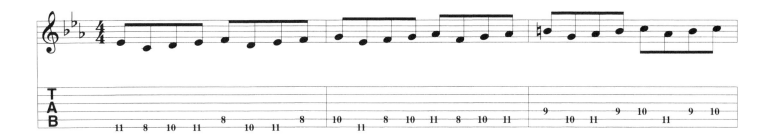

## Fingering #4

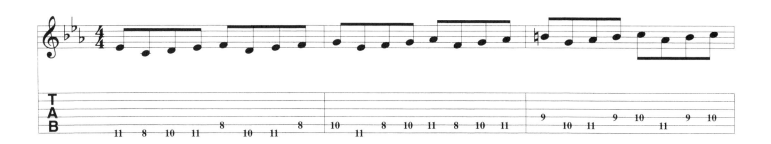

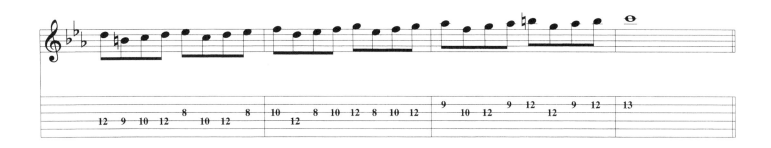

# Exercise #20: Scale Sequence in C Major

## Fingering #1

## Fingering #2

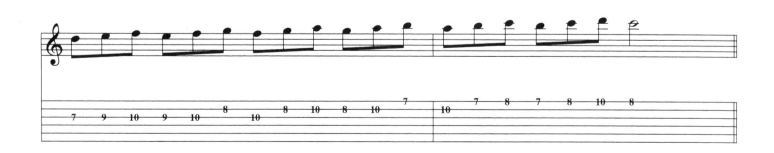

# Exercise #20: Scale Sequence in C Major

## Fingering #3

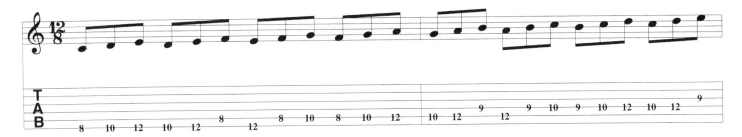

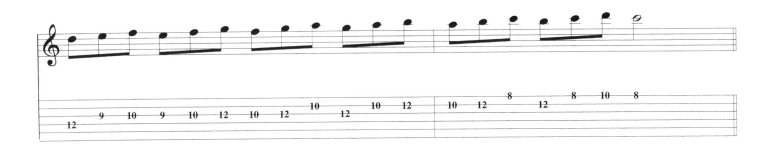

## Fingering #4

# Exercise #21: Scale Sequence in C Jazz Melodic Minor

## Fingering #1

## Fingering #2

# Exercise #21: Scale Sequence in C Jazz Melodic Minor

## Fingering #3

## Fingering #4

# Exercise #22: Scale Sequence in C Harmonic Minor

## Fingering #1

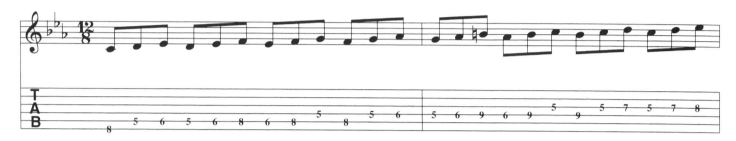

## Fingering #2

# Exercise #22: Scale Sequence in C Harmonic Minor

## Fingering #3

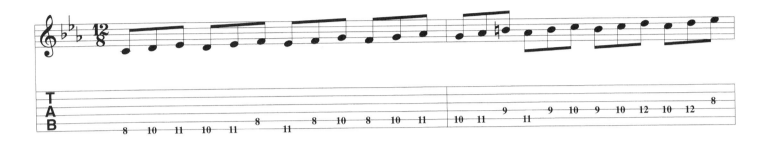

## Fingering #4

# Exercise #23: Scale Sequence in C Major

## Fingering #1

## Fingering #2

# Exercise #23: Scale Sequence in C Major

## Fingering #3

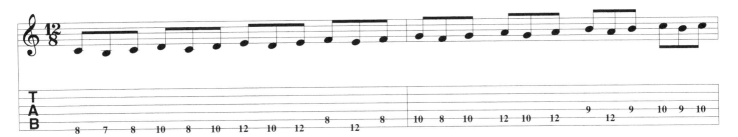

## Fingering #4

# Exercise #24: Scale Sequence in C Jazz Melodic Minor

## Fingering #1

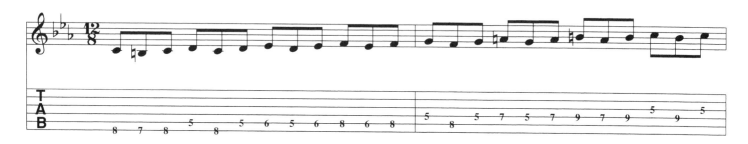

## Fingering #2

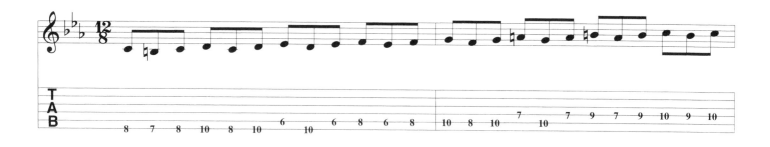

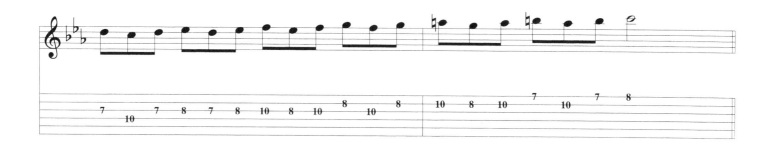

# Exercise #24: Scale Sequence in C Jazz Melodic Minor

## Fingering #3

## Fingering #4

# Exercise #25: Scale Sequence in C Harmonic Minor

## Fingering #1

## Fingering #2

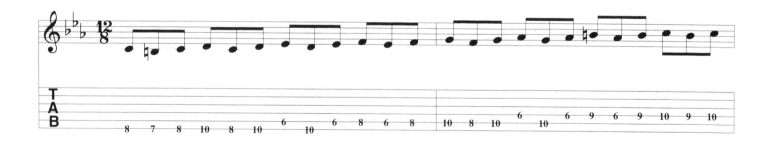

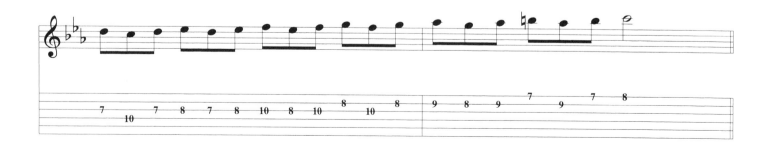

# Exercise #25: Scale Sequence in C Harmonic Minor

## Fingering #3

# Exercise #26: Scale Sequence in C Major

## Fingering #1

## Fingering #2

# Exercise #26: Scale Sequence in C Major

## Fingering #3

## Fingering #4

# Exercise #27: Scale Sequence in C Jazz Melodic Minor

## Fingering #1

## Fingering #2

# Exercise #27: Scale Sequence in C Jazz Melodic Minor

## Fingering #3

## Fingering #4

# Exercise #28: Scale Sequence in C Harmonic Minor

## Fingering #1

## Fingering #2

# Exercise #28: Scale Sequence in C Harmonic Minor

## Fingering #3

## Fingering #4

# Exercise #29: Ascending 3rds in C Jazz Melodic Minor

## Fingering #1

## Fingering #2

## Fingering #3

## Fingering #4

# Exercise #30: Ascending 3rds in C Jazz Melodic Minor

## Fingering #1

## Fingering #2

## Fingering #3

## Fingering #4

# Exercise #31: Ascending 3rds in C Harmonic Minor

## Fingering #1

## Fingering #2

## Fingering #3

## Fingering #4

# Exercise #32: Descending 3rds in C Major

## Fingering #1

## Fingering #2

## Fingering #3

## Fingering #4

# Exercise #33: Descending 3rds in C Jazz Melodic Minor

## Fingering #1

## Fingering #2

## Fingering #3

## Fingering #4

# Exercise #34: Descending 3rds in C Harmonic Minor

## Fingering #1

## Fingering #2

## Fingering #3

## Fingering #4

# Exercise #35: Descending 3rds in C Major

## Fingering #1

## Fingering #2

## Fingering #3

## Fingering #4

# Exercise #36: Descending 3rds in C Jazz Melodic Minor

## Fingering #1

## Fingering #2

## Fingering #3

## Fingering #4

# Exercise #37: Descending 3rds in C Harmonic Minor

## Fingering #1

## Fingering #2

## Fingering #3

## Fingering #4

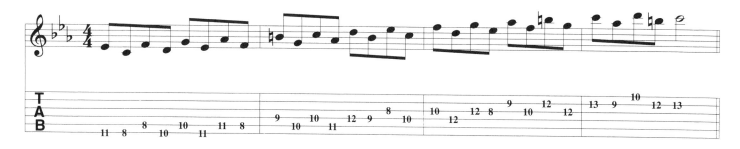

# Exercise #38: Ascending 3rds in C Major

## Fingering #1

## Fingering #2

## Fingering #3

## Fingering #4

# Exercise #39: Ascending 3rds in C Jazz Melodic Minor

## Fingering #1

## Fingering #2

## Fingering #3

## Fingering #4

# Exercise #40: Ascending 3rds in C Harmonic Minor

## Fingering #1

## Fingering #2

## Fingering #3

## Fingering #4

# Exercise #41: Ascending 4ths in C Major

## Fingering #1

## Fingering #2

## Fingering #3

## Fingering #4

# Exercise #42: Ascending 4ths in C Jazz Melodic Minor

## Fingering #1

## Fingering #2

## Fingering #3

## Fingering #4

# Exercise #43: Ascending 4ths in C Harmonic Minor

## Fingering #1

## Fingering #2

## Fingering #3

## Fingering #4

# Exercise #44: Descending 4ths in C Major

## Fingering #1

## Fingering #2

## Fingering #3

## Fingering #4

# Exercise #45: Descending 4ths in C Jazz Melodic Minor

## Fingering #1

## Fingering #2

## Fingering #3

## Fingering #4

# Exercise #46: Descending 4ths in C Harmonic Minor

## Fingering #1

## Fingering #2

## Fingering #3

## Fingering #4

# Exercise #47: Descending 4ths in C Major

## Fingering #1

## Fingering #2

## Fingering #3

## Fingering #4

# Exercise #48: Descending 4ths in C Jazz Melodic Minor

## Fingering #1

## Fingering #2

## Fingering #3

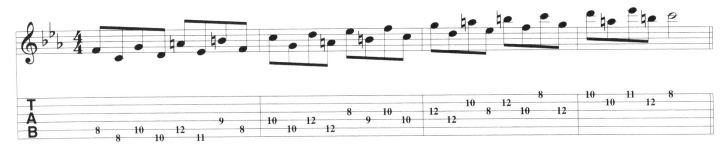

## Fingering #4

# Exercise #49: Descending 4ths in C Harmonic Minor

## Fingering #1

## Fingering #2

## Fingering #3

## Fingering #4

# Exercise #50: Ascending 4ths in C Major

## Fingering #1

## Fingering #2

## Fingering #3

## Fingering #4

# Exercise #51: Ascending 4ths in C Jazz Melodic Minor

## Fingering #1

## Fingering #2

## Fingering #3

## Fingering #4

# Exercise #52: Ascending 4ths in C Harmonic Minor

## Fingering #1

## Fingering #2

## Fingering #3

## Fingering #4

# Exercise #53: Ascending 5ths in C Major

## Fingering #1

## Fingering #2

## Fingering #3

## Fingering #4

# Exercise #54: Ascending 5ths in C Jazz Melodic Minor

## Fingering #1

## Fingering #2

## Fingering #3

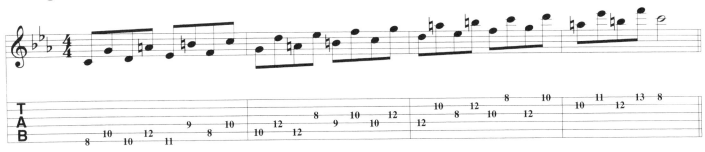

## Fingering #4

# Exercise #55: Ascending 5ths in C Harmonic Minor

## Fingering #1

## Fingering #2

## Fingering #3

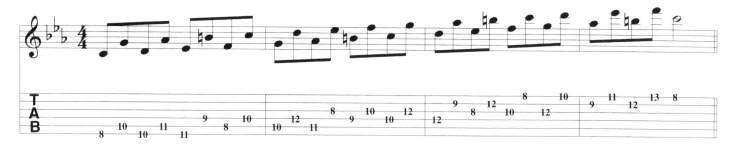

## Fingering #4

# Exercise #56: Descending 5ths in C Major

## Fingering #1

## Fingering #2

## Fingering #3

## Fingering #4

# Exercise #57: Descending 5ths in C Jazz Melodic Minor

## Fingering #1

## Fingering #2

## Fingering #3

## Fingering #4

# Exercise #58: Descending 5ths in C Harmonic Minor

## Fingering #1

## Fingering #2

## Fingering #3

## Fingering #4

# Exercise #59: Descending 5ths in C Major

## Fingering #1

## Fingering #2

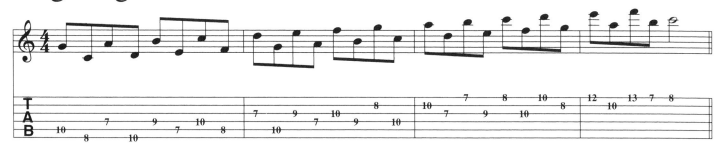

## Fingering #3

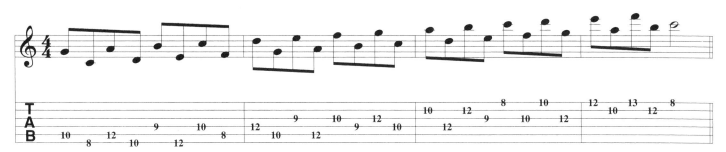

## Fingering #4

# Exercise #60: Descending 5ths in C Jazz Melodic Minor

## Fingering #1

## Fingering #2

## Fingering  #3

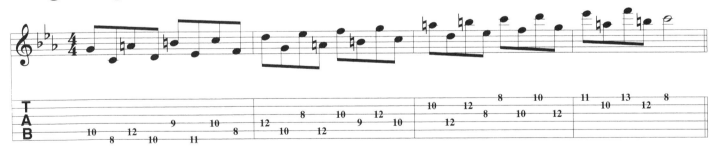

## Fingering #4

# Exercise #61: Descending 5ths in C Harmonic Minor

## Fingering #1

## Fingering #2

## Fingering #3

## Fingering #4

# Exercise #62: Ascending 5ths in C Major

## Fingering #1

## Fingering #2

## Fingering #3

## Fingering #4

# Exercise #63: Ascending 5ths in C Jazz Melodic Minor

## Fingering #1

## Fingering #2

## Fingering #3

## Fingering #4

# Exercise #64: Ascending 5ths in C Harmonic Minor

## Fingering #1

## Fingering #2

## Fingering #3

## Fingering #4

# Exercise #65: Ascending 6ths in C Major

## Fingering #1

## Fingering #2

## Fingering #3

## Fingering #4

# Exercise #66: Ascending 6ths in C Jazz Melodic Minor

## Fingering #1

## Fingering #2

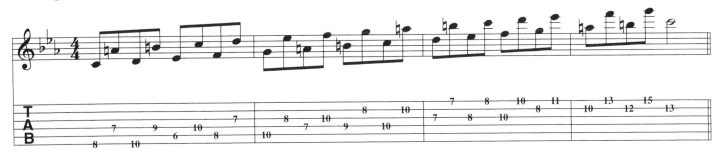

## Fingering #3

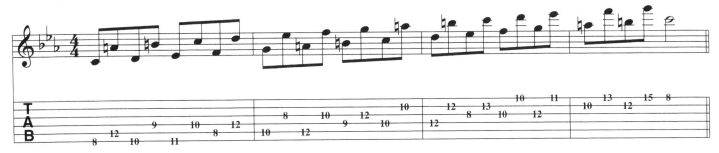

## Fingering #4

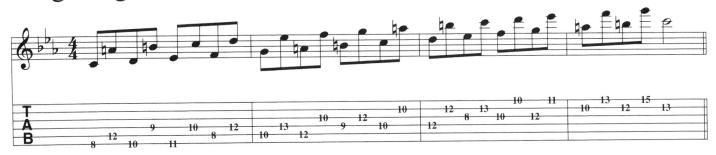

# Exercise #67: Ascending 6ths in C Harmonic Minor

## Fingering #1

## Fingering #2

## Fingering #3

## Fingering #4

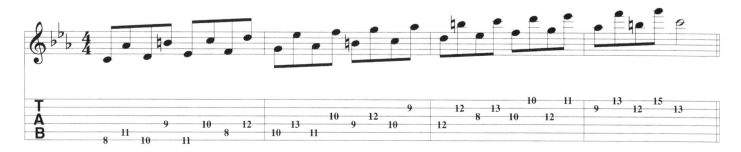

# Exercise #68: Descending 6ths in C Major

## Fingering #1

## Fingering #2

## Fingering #3

## Fingering #4

# Exercise #69: Descending 6ths in C Jazz Melodic Minor

## Fingering #1

## Fingering #2

## Fingering #3

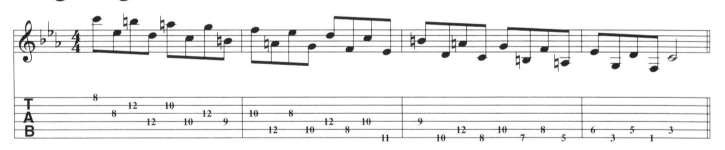

## Fingering #4

# Exercise #70: Descending 6ths in C Harmonic Minor

## Fingering #1

## Fingering #2

## Fingering #3

## Fingering #4

# Exercise #71: Descending 6ths in C Major

## Fingering #1

## Fingering #2

## Fingering #3

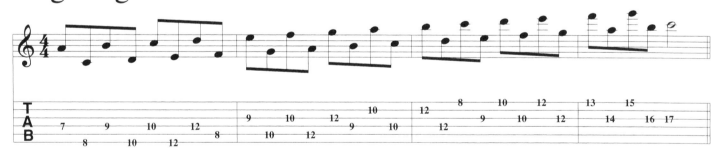

## Fingering #4

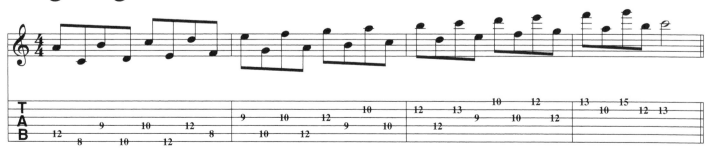

# Exercise #72: Descending 6ths in C Jazz Melodic Minor

## Fingering #1

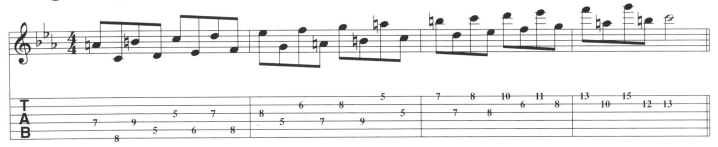

## Fingering #2

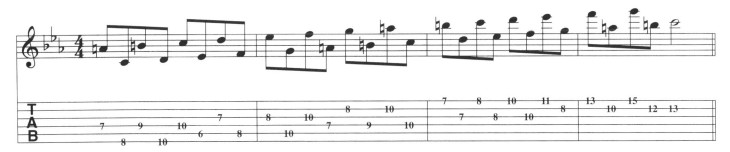

## Fingering #3

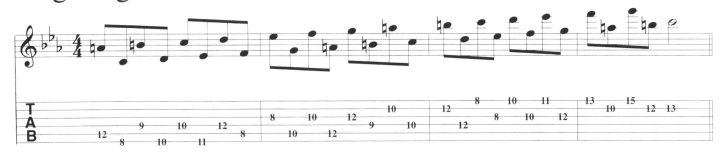

## Fingering #4

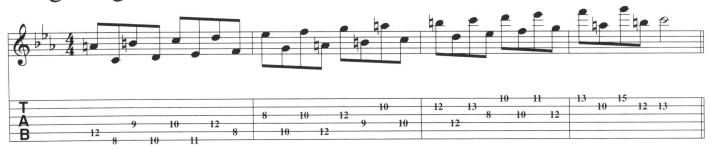

# Exercise #73: Descending 6ths in C Harmonic Minor

## Fingering #1

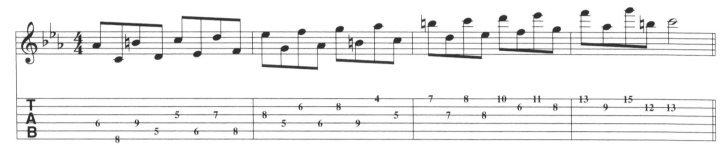

## Fingering #2

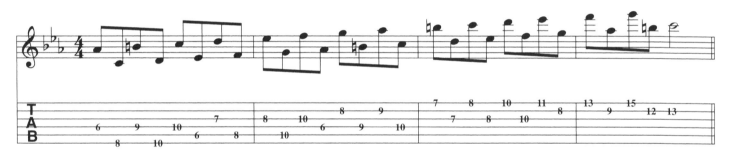

## Fingering #3

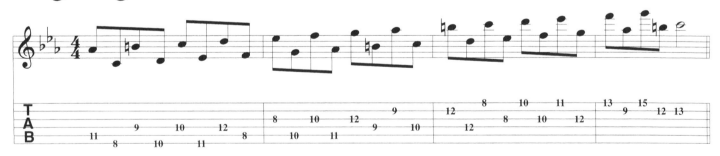

## Fingering #4

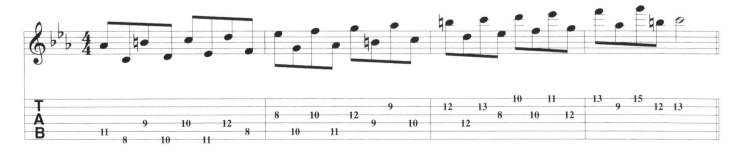

# Exercise #74: Ascending 6ths in C Major

## Fingering #1

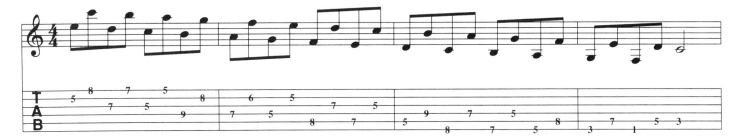

## Fingering #2

## Fingering #3

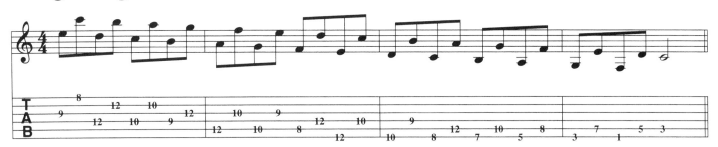

## Fingering #4

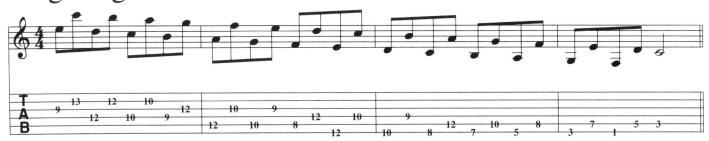

# Exercise #75: Ascending 6ths in C Jazz Melodic Minor

## Fingering #1

## Fingering #2

## Fingering #3

## Fingering #4

# Exercise #76: Ascending 7ths in C Major

## Fingering #1

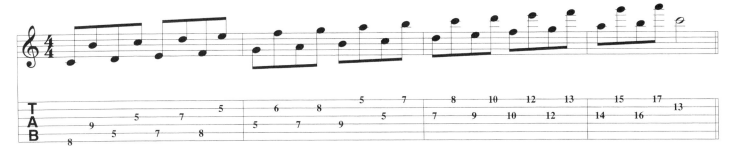

## Fingering #2

## Fingering #3

## Fingering #4

# Exercise #77: Ascending 7ths in C Jazz Melodic Minor

## Fingering #1

## Fingering #2

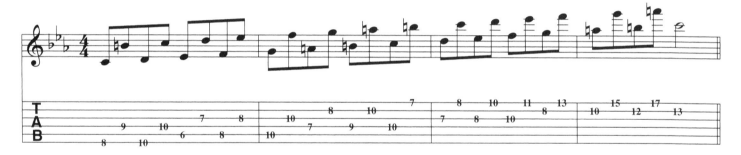

## Fingering #3

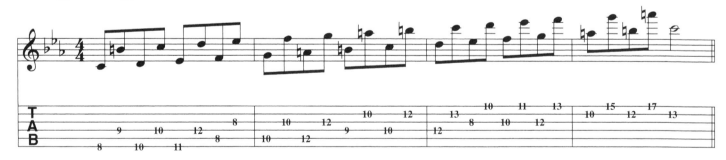

## Fingering #4

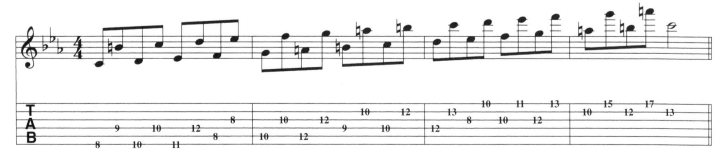

# Exercise #78: Ascending 7ths in C Harmonic Minor

## Fingering #1

## Fingering #2

## Fingering #3

## Fingering #4

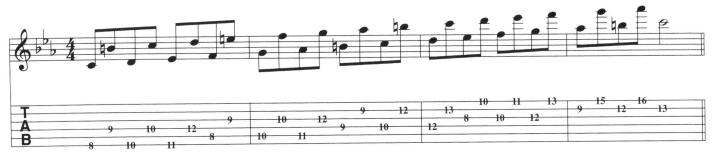

# Exercise #79: Descending 7ths in C Major

## Fingering #1

## Fingering #2

## Fingering #3

## Fingering #4

# Exercise #80: Descending 7ths in C Jazz Melodic Minor

## Fingering #1

## Fingering #2

## Fingering #3

## Fingering #4

# Exercise #81: Descending 7ths in C Harmonic Minor

## Fingering #1

## Fingering #2

## Fingering #3

## Fingering #4

# Exercise #82: Descending 7ths in C Major

## Fingering #1

## Fingering #2

## Fingering #3

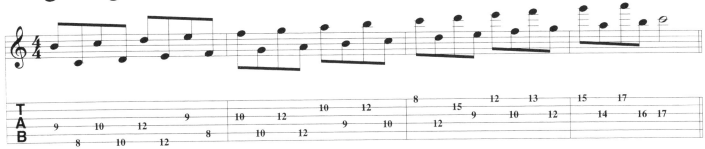

## Fingering #4

# Exercise #83: Descending 7ths in C Jazz Melodic Minor

## Fingering #1

## Fingering #2

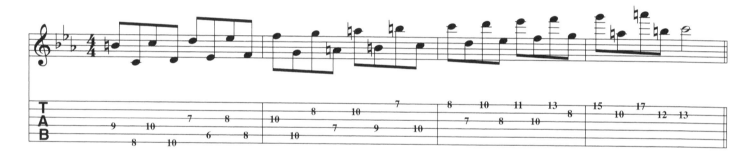

## Fingering #3

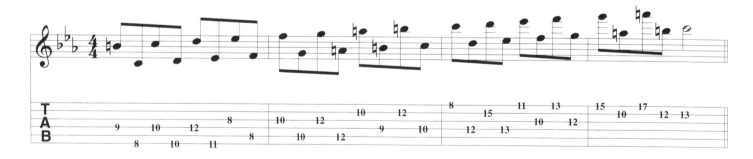

## Fingering #4

# Exercise #84: Descending 7ths in C Harmonic Minor

## Fingering #1

## Fingering #2

## Fingering #3

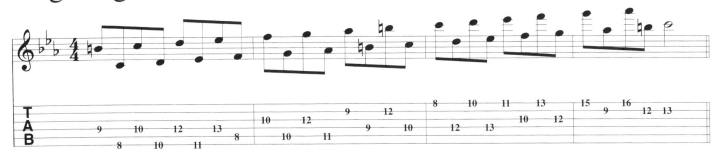

## Fingering #4

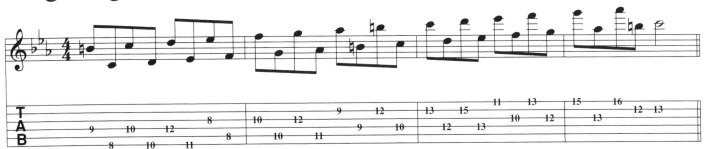

# Exercise #85: Ascending 7ths in C Major

## Fingering #1

## Fingering #2

## Fingering #3

# Exercise #86: Ascending 7ths in C Jazz Melodic Minor

## Fingering #1

## Fingering #2

## Fingering #3

## Fingering #4

# Exercise #87: Ascending 7ths in C Harmonic Minor

## Fingering #1

## Fingering #2

## Fingering #3

## Fingering #4

# Exercise #88: C Arpeggio

## Fingering #1

## Fingering #2

## Fingering #3

## Fingering #4

# Exercise #89: Cm Arpeggio

## Fingering #1

## Fingering #2

## Fingering #3

## Fingering #4

# Exercise #90: Caug Arpeggio

## Fingering #1

## Fingering #2

## Fingering #3

## Fingering #4

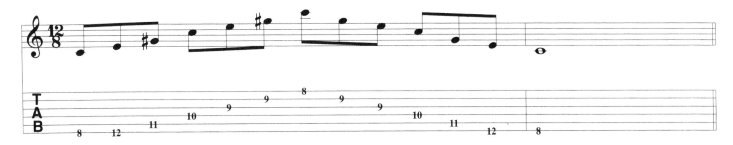

# Exercise #91: Cdim Arpeggio

## Fingering #1

## Fingering #2

## Fingering #3

## Fingering #4

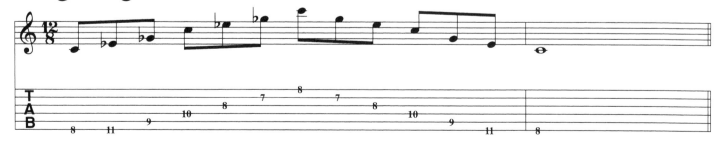

# Exercise #92: Csus4 Arpeggio

## Fingering #1

## Fingering #2

## Fingering #3

## Fingering #4

# Exercise #93: Csus2 Arpeggio

## Fingering #1

## Fingering #2

## Fingering #3

## Fingering #4

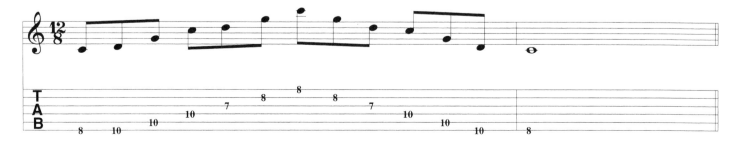

# Exercise #94: Cadd9 Arpeggio

## Fingering #1

## Fingering #2

## Fingering #3

## Fingering #4

# Exercise #95: Cmadd9 Arpeggio

## Fingering #1

## Fingering #2

## Fingering #3

## Fingering #4

# Exercise #96: C6 Arpeggio

## Fingering #1

## Fingering #2

## Fingering #3

## Fingering #4

# Exercise #97: Cm6 Arpeggio

## Fingering #1

## Fingering #2

## Fingering #3

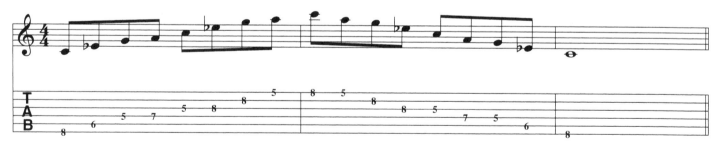

## Fingering #4

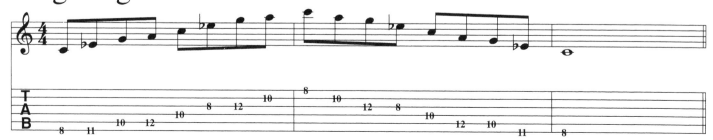

# Exercise #98: Cmaj7 Arpeggio

## Fingering #1

## Fingering #2

## Fingering #3

## Fingering #4

# Exercise #99: C7 Arpeggio

## Fingering #1

## Fingering #2

## Fingering #3

## Fingering #4

# Exercise #100: Cm7 Arpeggio

## Fingering #1

## Fingering #2

## Fingering #3

## Fingering #4

# Exercise #101: Cmaj7♯5 Arpeggio

## Fingering #1

## Fingering #2

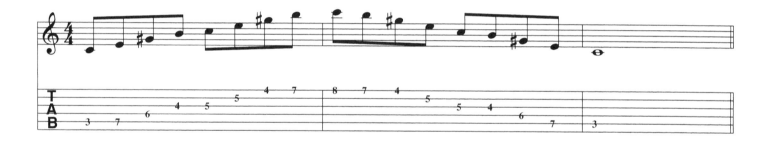

## Fingering #3

## Fingering #4

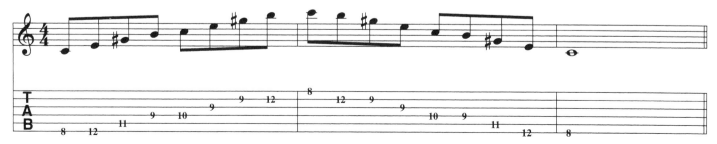

# Exercise #102: Cmaj7♭5 Arpeggio

## Fingering #1

## Fingering #2

## Fingering #3

## Fingering #4

# Exercise #103: C7♯5 Arpeggio

## Fingering #1

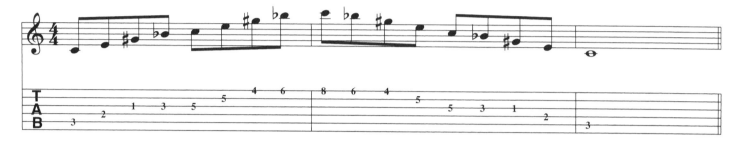

## Fingering #2

## Fingering #3

## Fingering #4

# Exercise #104: C7♭5 Arpeggio

## Fingering #1

## Fingering #2

## Fingering #3

## Fingering #4

# Exercise #105: Cm7♭5 Arpeggio

## Fingering #1

## Fingering #2

## Fingering #3

## Fingering #4

# Exercise #106: Cm/maj7 Arpeggio

## Fingering #1

## Fingering #2

## Fingering #3

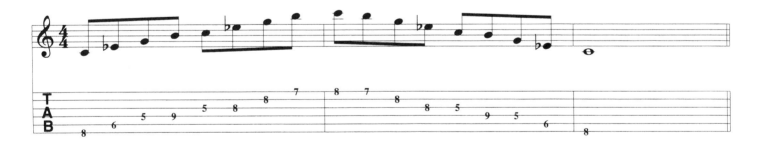

## Fingering #4

# Exercise #107: Cdim7 Arpeggio

## Fingering #1

## Fingering #2

## Fingering #3

## Fingering #4

# Exercise #108: Cm/maj7♭5 Arpeggio

## Fingering #1

## Fingering #2

## Fingering #3

## Fingering #4

# Exercise #109: C Arpeggio Sequence

## Fingering #1

## Fingering #2

## Fingering #3

## Fingering #4

# Exercise #110: Cm Arpeggio Sequence

## Fingering #1

## Fingering #2

## Fingering #3

## Fingering #4

# Exercise #111: Caug Arpeggio Sequence

## Fingering #1

## Fingering #2

## Fingering #3

## Fingering #4

# Exercise #112: Cdim Arpeggio Sequence

## Fingering #1

## Fingering #2

## Fingering #3

## Fingering #4

# Exercise #113: Csus4 Arpeggio Sequence

## Fingering #1

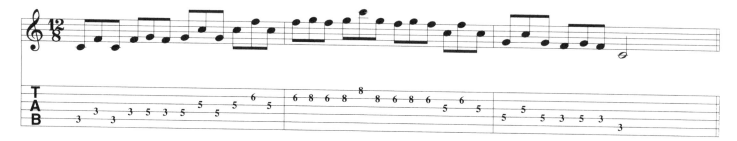

## Fingering #2

## Fingering #3

## Fingering #4

# Exercise #114: Csus2 Arpeggio Sequence

## Fingering #1

## Fingering #2

## Fingering #3

## Fingering #4

# Exercise #115: Cadd9 Arpeggio Sequence

## Fingering #1

## Fingering #2

# Exercise #115: Cadd9 Arpeggio Sequence

## Fingering #3

## Fingering #4

# Exercise #116: Cmadd9 Arpeggio Sequence

## Fingering #1

## Fingering #2

# Exercise #116: Cmadd9 Arpeggio Sequence

## Fingering #3

## Fingering #4

# Exercise #117: C6 Arpeggio Sequence

## Fingering #1

## Fingering #2

# Exercise #117: C6 Arpeggio Sequence

## Fingering #3

## Fingering #4

# Exercise #118: Cm6 Arpeggio Sequence

## Fingering #1

## Fingering #2

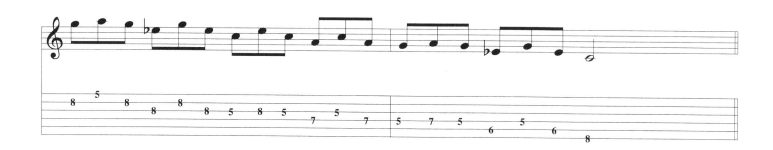

# Exercise #118: Cm6 Arpeggio Sequence

## Fingering #3

# Exercise #119: Cmaj7 Arpeggio Sequence

## Fingering #1

## Fingering #2

# Exercise #119: Cmaj7 Arpeggio Sequence

## Fingering #3

## Fingering #4

# Exercise #120: C7 Arpeggio Sequence

## Fingering #1

## Fingering #2

# Exercise #120: C7 Arpeggio Sequence

## Fingering #3

## Fingering #4

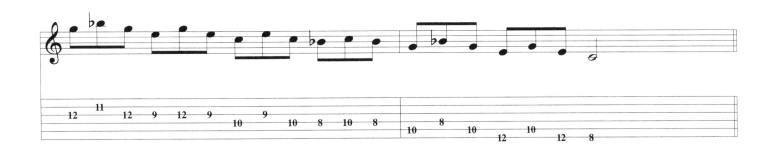

# Exercise #121: Cm7 Arpeggio Sequence

## Fingering #1

## Fingering #2

# Exercise #121: Cm7 Arpeggio Sequence

## Fingering #3

## Fingering #4

# Exercise #122: Cmaj7♯5 Arpeggio Sequence

## Fingering #1

## Fingering #2

# Exercise #122: Cmaj7♯5 Arpeggio Sequence

## Fingering #3

## Fingering #4

# Exercise #123: Cmaj7♭5 Arpeggio Sequence

## Fingering #1

## Fingering #2

# Exercise #123: Cmaj7♭5 Arpeggio Sequence

## Fingering #3

## Fingering #4

# Exercise #124: C7♯5 Arpeggio Sequence

## Fingering #1

## Fingering #2

# Exercise #124: C7♯5 Arpeggio Sequence

## Fingering #3

## Fingering #4

# Exercise #125: C7♭5 Arpeggio Sequence

## Fingering #1

## Fingering #2

# Exercise #125: C7♭5 Arpeggio Sequence

## Fingering #3

## Fingering #4

# Exercise #126: Cm7♭5 Arpeggio Sequence

## Fingering #1

## Fingering #2

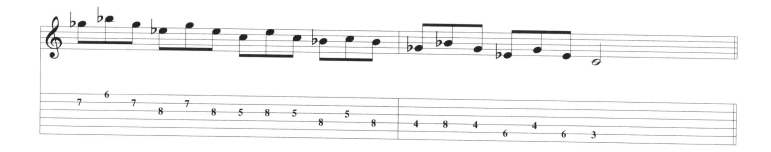

# Exercise #126: Cm7♭5 Arpeggio Sequence

## Fingering #3

## Fingering #4

# Exercise #127: Cm/maj7 Arpeggio Sequence

## Fingering #1

## Fingering #2

# Exercise #127: Cm/maj7 Arpeggio Sequence

## Fingering #3

## Fingering #4

# Exercise #128: Cdim7 Arpeggio Sequence

## Fingering #1

## Fingering #2

# Exercise #128: Cdim7 Arpeggio Sequence

## Fingering #3

## Fingering #4

# Exercise #129: Cm/maj7♭5 Arpeggio Sequence

## Fingering #1

## Fingering #2

# Exercise #129: Cm/maj7♭5 Arpeggio Sequence

## Fingering #3

## Fingering #4

# Exercise #130: C Arpeggio Sequence

## Fingering #1

## Fingering #2

## Fingering #3

## Fingering #4

# Exercise #131: Cm Arpeggio Sequence

## Fingering #1

## Fingering #2

## Fingering #3

## Fingering #4

# Exercise #132: Caug Arpeggio Sequence

## Fingering #1

## Fingering #2

## Fingering #3

## Fingering #4

# Exercise #133: Cdim Arpeggio Sequence

## Fingering #1

## Fingering #2

## Fingering  #3

## Fingering #4

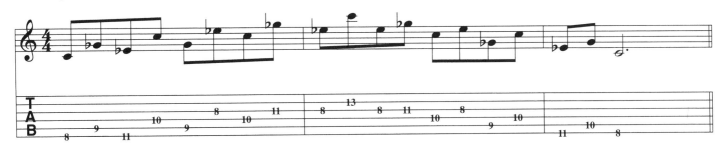

# Exercise #134: Csus4 Arpeggio Sequence

## Fingering #1

## Fingering #2

## Fingering #3

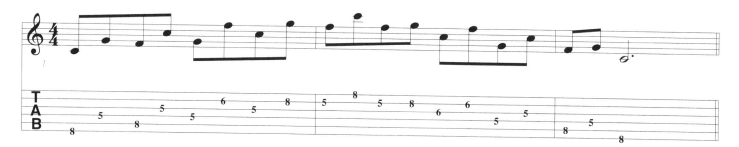

## Fingering #4

# Exercise #135: Csus2 Arpeggio Sequence

## Fingering #1

## Fingering #2

## Fingering #3

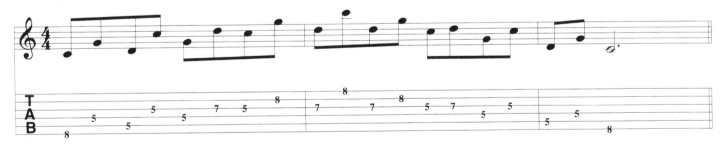

## Fingering #4

# Exercise #136: Cadd9 Arpeggio Sequence

## Fingering #1

## Fingering #2

## Fingering #3

## Fingering #4

# Exercise #137: Cmadd9 Arpeggio Sequence

## Fingering #1

## Fingering #2

## Fingering #3

## Fingering #4

# Exercise #138: C6 Arpeggio Sequence

## Fingering #1

## Fingering #2

## Fingering #3

## Fingering #4

# Exercise #139: Cm6 Arpeggio Sequence

## Fingering #1

## Fingering #2

## Fingering #3

## Fingering #4

# Exercise #140: Cmaj7 Arpeggio Sequence

## Fingering #1

## Fingering #2

## Fingering #3

## Fingering #4

# Exercise #141: C7 Arpeggio Sequence

## Fingering #1

## Fingering #2

## Fingering #3

## Fingering #4

## Exercise #142: Cm7 Arpeggio Sequence

## Fingering #1

## Fingering #2

## Fingering #3

## Fingering #4

# Exercise #143: Cmaj7♯5 Arpeggio Sequence

## Fingering #1

## Fingering #2

## Fingering #3

## Fingering #4

# Exercise #144: Cmaj7♭5 Arpeggio Sequence

## Fingering #1

## Fingering #2

## Fingering #3

## Fingering #4

# Exercise #145: C7♯5 Arpeggio Sequence

## Fingering #1

## Fingering #2

## Fingering #3

## Fingering #4

# Exercise #146: C7♭5 Arpeggio Sequence

## Fingering #1

## Fingering #2

## Fingering #3

## Fingering #4

# Exercise #147: Cm7♭5 Arpeggio Sequence

## Fingering #1

## Fingering #2

## Fingering #3

## Fingering #4

# Exercise #148: Cm/maj7 Arpeggio Sequence

## Fingering #1

## Fingering #2

## Fingering #3

## Fingering #4

# Exercise #149: Cdim7 Arpeggio Sequence

## Fingering #1

## Fingering #2

## Fingering #3

## Fingering #4

# Exercise #150: Cm/maj7♭5 Arpeggio Sequence

## Fingering #1

## Fingering #2

## Fingering #3

## Fingering #4

# Exercise #151: Diatonic Arpeggio Sequence in C Major

## Fingering #1

## Fingering #2

# Exercise #151: Diatonic Arpeggio Sequence in C Major

## Fingering #3

## Fingering #4

# Exercise #152: Diatonic Arpeggio Sequence in C Major

## Fingering #1

## Fingering #2

# Exercise #152: Diatonic Arpeggio Sequence in C Major

## Fingering #3

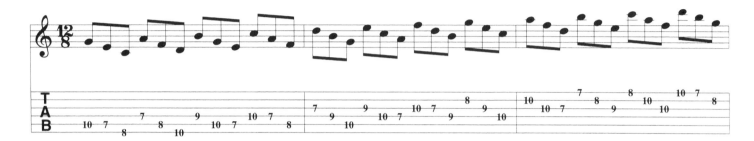

## Fingering #4

# Exercise #153: Diatonic Arpeggio Sequence in C Major

## Fingering #1

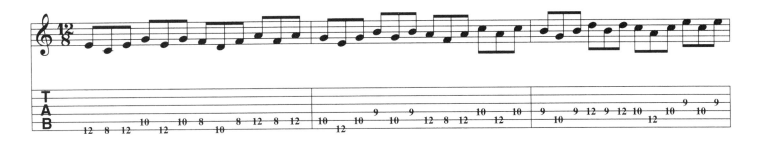

## Fingering #2

# Exercise #153: Diatonic Arpeggio Sequence in C Major

## Fingering #3

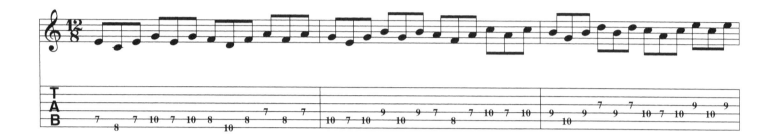

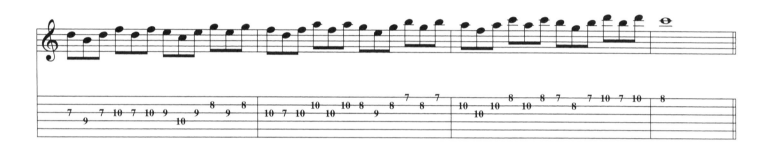

## Fingering #4

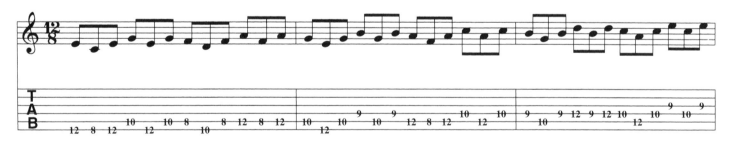

# Exercise #154: Diatonic Arpeggio Sequence in C Major

## Fingering #1

## Fingering #2

# Exercise #154: Diatonic Arpeggio Sequence in C Major

## Fingering #3

## Fingering #4

# Exercise #155: Diatonic Arpeggio Sequence in C Major

## Fingering #1

## Fingering #2

# Exercise #155: Diatonic Arpeggio Sequence in C Major

## Fingering #3

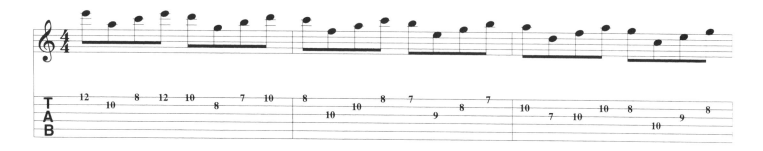

## Fingering #4

# Exercise #156: Diatonic Arpeggio Sequence in C Major

## Fingering #1

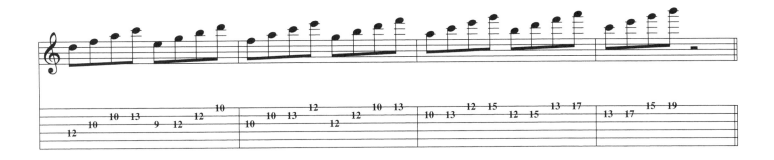

## Fingering #2

# Exercise #156: Diatonic Arpeggio Sequence in C Major

## Fingering #3

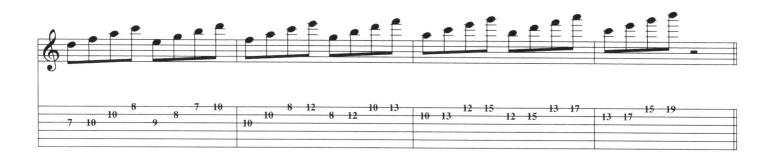

## Fingering #4

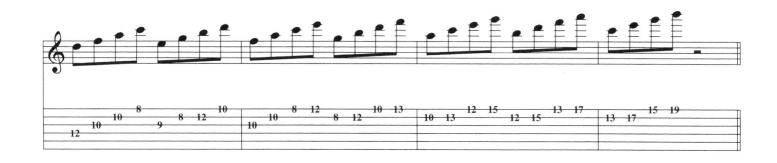

# Exercise #157: Diatonic Arpeggio Sequence in C Major

## Fingering #1

## Fingering #2

## Fingering #3

## Fingering #4

# Exercise #158: Linear Diatonic Arpeggios in C Major

## #1

## #2

# Exercise #159: Linear Diatonic Arpeggios in C Major

**#1**

**#2**

**#3**

**#4**

## J.S Bach Sonata #5 Allegro Assai

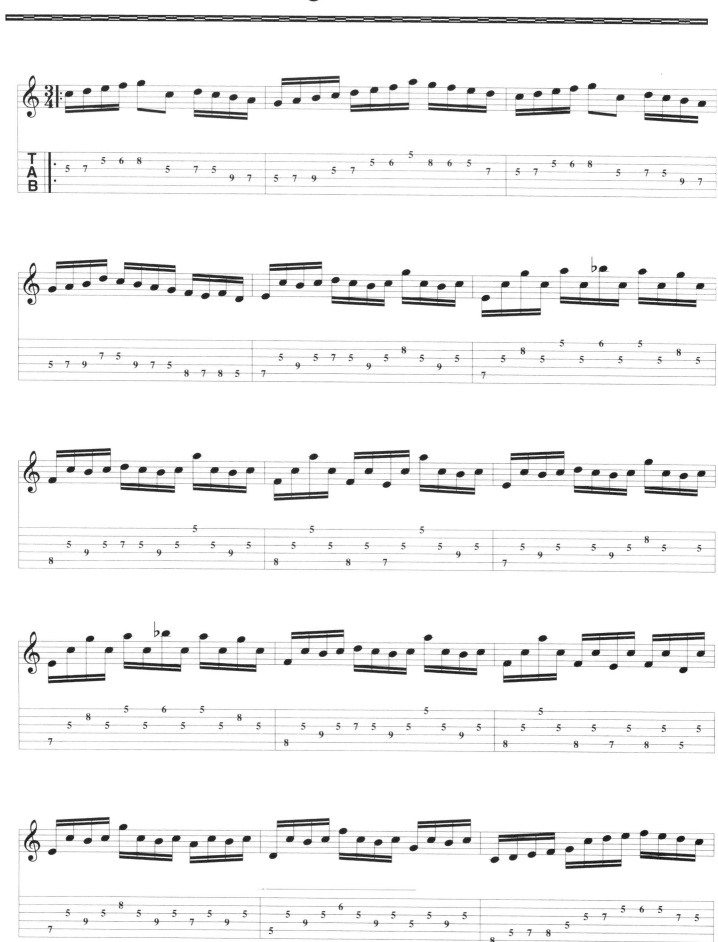

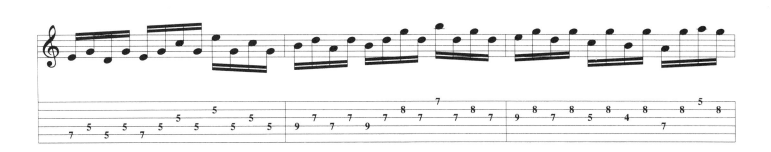

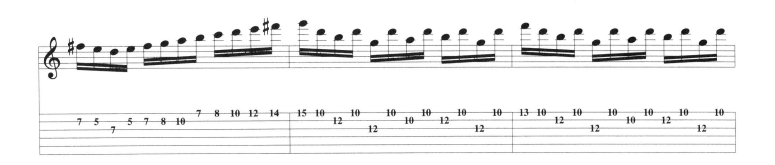

# Paganini Moto Perpetuo

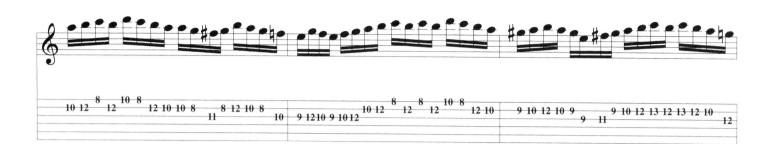

2.

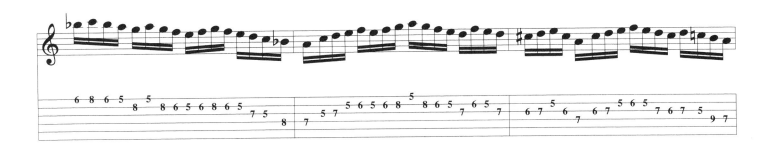

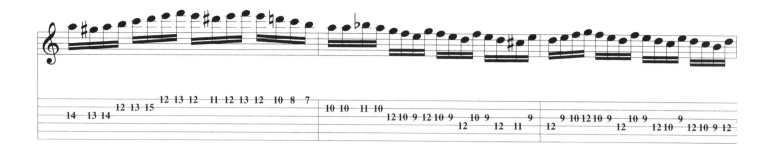

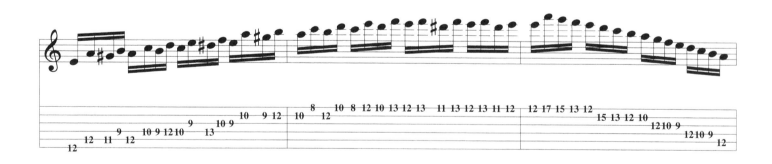

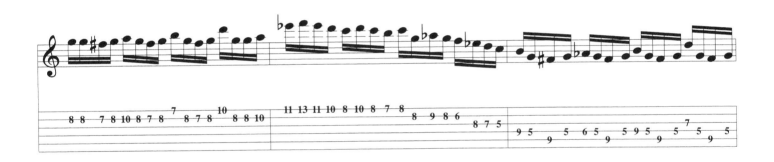

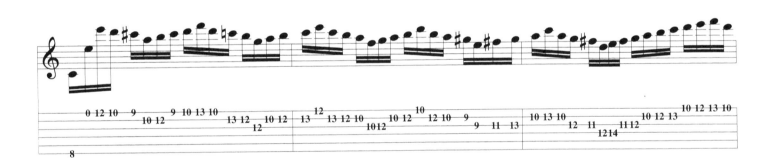

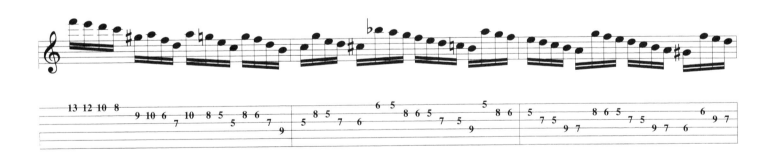

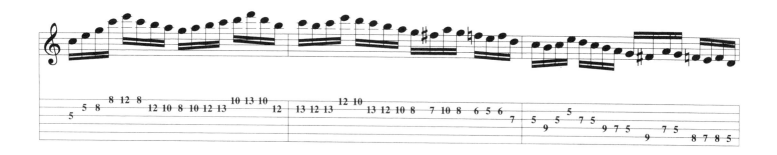

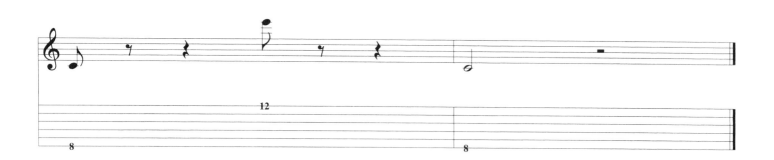

# Wohlfahrt Study #3 Moderato